NANO AND NICKI IN BOCA RATON

Sherry Kramer

BROADWAY PLAY PUBLISHING INC
New York
www.broadwayplaypub.com
info@broadwayplaypub.com

NANO AND NICKI IN BOCA RATON
© Copyright 2013 by Sherry Kramer

First printing: April 2013
I S B N: 978-0-88145-549-6

Book design: Marie Donovan
Page make-up: Adobe Indesign
Typeface: Palatino
Printed and bound in the U S A

CHARACTERS & SETTING

NANO, *everything about her is elegant. She is 84 years old, majored in Latin in college. Has always had money. Lives in Kansas City. Doesn't have a southern accent or a northern one—she is that rare species known as an almost Southern Jew. Knows not one word of Yiddish.*

Nano still has all her hair—it's a pure silver white, and is always beautifully in place. She keeps all her jewelry in the vault, and wears only a gold wrist watch and her wedding ring. She dresses in a black wool suit with a box jacket. A red silk scarf knotted around her neck, tucked in carefully. Her shoes are slightly boxy. Her nails are long, and perfectly manicured.

At night, she wears a matching pink fleece nightgown and robe set. She wears a satin pink hair protector that NICKI *calls her helmet—it is a more or less rectangular piece of satin with a velcro closure.*

NICKI, *her granddaughter. Almost a foot taller than her grandmother. Lives in New York, after a Seven Sisters education. She is 30 years old.*

She dresses in a style born of compromise—her flowing flower child mentality, combined with NANO's *rigid perception of what a young lady should wear. As a general rule, the result is a mid-calf length jean skirt and a Mexican peasant blouse, with a pair of leather sandals that* NANO *would have thrown out last year.*

At night, she wears a sexy, black nightgown that NANO *has just bought her.*

THE MAID, *a woman in her 50s. Non-speaking role.*

A progression of Howard Johnson motel rooms.

Time: 1984

Scene One

(Preshow: The maid is making up an ordinary Howard Johnson's motel room.)

(She pushes her maid's cart along, humming Meet Me In Saint Louis, Louis.*)*

(As the house lights fade, she places a WELCOME TO SAINT LOUIS SIGN—*one of those high gloss tent placards— on top of the T V, and exits through the door.)*

(A beat)

(The sound of a key turning in the lock of the door.)

(We hear NANO*'s voice from the hallway, from the other side of the door.)*

NANO: *(O S)* Do you really think two women traveling alone should be on the ground floor? *(As the door opens a few inches)* I don't know, Nicki, two women, all alone— *(The door slams shut.)*

(A beat)

(The key is turning again.)

NANO: Now as soon as we get in I want you to look at the map they've got on the back of the door and show me where to get out if there's a fire. Ouuuuuuh, I hate being up so high, I feel trapped— *(The door opens slightly.)* —I know you'll be with me, but— *(The door is immediately shut.)*

(The sound of the key in the lock.)

Oh, Nicki, I'm sure we'll be fine here—you're not going running to that damn manager again—so what if this room is way out in the boondocks, at the very end of the world, I know how to scream real loud— *(The door opens.)* —and you know how to run— *(The door closes slowly.)*

(A beat)

*(The sound of the key in the door—and the door is flung open—*NICKI *rushes into the bathroom, and* NANO *throws herself onto the bed nearest the door.)*

NANO: You hurry or I won't be responsible. Ooooooh, I'm dead. Dead. Dead. Dead.

NICKI: *(She flushes the toilet.)* All yours. *(She comes out of the bathroom, carrying two wrapped bars of motel soap.)*

NANO: *(Hoists herself off the bed and hobbles, obviously holding it in, to the bathroom.)* Don't you go stealing all the soap, leaving me without any.

NICKI: *(As she puts their overnight bags on the luggage stand, she slips the soap into her bag.)* You bring your own soap anyway.

NANO: So, that doesn't mean I might not want to use some of theirs occasionally. *(She goes into the bathroom, leaving the door slightly open.)* I'll never forget the time you were over at our house and you came out of the bathroom with your plastic training pants draggin' almost to the floor—you were just a little bit of a thing—and I said to myself, Good Lord, she's got a full load in there.

NICKI: *(As she goes through the room, opening up drawers, taking out the stationary and putting it in her overnight bag, and looking through all the brochures.)* I've never really believed that story, Nano.

NANO: *(O S)* So I got you right back into that bathroom real quick and if you hadn't stuffed your panties all

full of bars of soap. Said you were taking 'em home
to your mother and father cause they didn't have any.
(She laughs softly to herself.) Imagine. Two years old
and even then you couldn't keep your hands off other
people's soap.

NICKI: I like the one about walking in on Uncle Harry
better.

NANO: *(O S)* Yes, that was something—he wasn't used
to children, and he didn't bother locking the door—
you marched in, unannounced— scared him more than
it did you. I'll never forget the way you came up to
me, with the saddest look on your face and said "Poor
Uncle Harry. Nobody taught him how to tinkle."
There's a shower cap in here wrapped in plastic, you
want it?

NICKI: Nope, don't use 'em.

NANO: *(O S)* Someone might. Your mother.

NICKI: Yeah, okay, remind me. *(She picks up the ice
bucket from the counter.)* Hey, Nano, this is just exactly
the right size for that planter that leaks—you've been
looking for a liner, this will be perfect.

NANO: *(O S)* What will?

NICKI: The ice bucket. For your planter. I'll put it in my
suitcase. *(She does.)*

NANO: *(O S)* You will do no such thing.

NICKI: But—

NANO: *(O S)* That is stealing.

NICKI: But—

NANO: *(O S)* Put it back.

NICKI: *(Sighs, shakes her head, and puts it back. She unlocks
the sliding glass door, opens it, and steps, out onto the*

balcony. Sounds of traffic drift into the room.) Oh, great. Right over the lobby.

NANO: *(O S)* Nicki?...did you open a window? CLOSE THAT WINDOW!!!!!! THERE'S A DRAFT!

NICKI: *(Stepping inside and quickly slamming the door shut)* There is not. And even if there were, it couldn't of gotten all the way from here to where you could have felt it half that fast.

NANO: *(O S)* I shall let you know, Nicki, when I am too old to know what I feel.

NICKI: Princess and the Pea.

NANO: *(O S)* What?

NICKI: NOTHING.

NANO: *(O S)* You think everybody should be Nanoock of the North, like you. Well, they shouldn't. I appreciate a nice warm room. I remember the days before central heating.

NICKI: Well, you're sure making up for lost time now. Remember last year, when you forgot to turn down the thermostat before we left for Boca? We got back, and your kitchen was covered with mold. Took your girl five days with Clorox and a toothbrush to get it all off. Good thing it didn't get into the Persians—it would have taken a flame thrower to get it out.

NANO: *(O S)* Oh, stop it, Nicki. I keep my house comfortable. Why shouldn't I?

NICKI: Would have made one fabulous sitcom. *(Uses booming announcer type voice)* "Eighty-four year old grandmother of three turns French provincial home into disease control center after rare mold cultures coat every stick of furniture in the place. In tonight's thrilling episode of HAVE MOLD, WILL SWEAT

HERE, Nano grows the cure for cancer in the Louis the 14th love seats."

NANO: *(O S)* Do you want this shower cap or don't you?

NICKI: Okay, sure, I'll take it.

NANO: *(O S. The sound of the toilet flushing)* Lookie here— *(She enters from the bathroom, carrying the shower cap, and several courtesy bottles of shampoo, conditioner, and lotion.)* Aren't these nice—

(NANO shows them to NICKI.)

NICKI: I'll take the shampoo, it's the kind I use. *(She takes the shampoo and puts it in her overnight bag.)*

NANO: No, take 'em all.

NICKI: But don't you want the handcreme? In case you run out?

NANO: I'm up to my ears in lotions, Nicki. Here—you take 'em.

NICKI: Well, if you're sure. *(She puts everything in her overnight bag.)*

(The sound of a souped-up car racing its engine, then peeling away fills the room.)

NANO: What's that noise—is somebody trying to get in?

NICKI: They gave us a room right over the lobby. We'll hear them driving up and checking in and pulling out all night.

NANO: They see two women traveling alone and they figure they'll stick us with the worst room in the place.

NICKI: They didn't do it intentionally, Nano—

NANO: They wouldn't have dared do it to your grandfather.

NICKI: People are not out to get us because we're women, Nano. They're out to get us because they're out to get everybody. It has nothing to do with us. We gave them an opportunity to get us and they took it. You think they get some special pleasure from giving us an awful room? No, Nano, they get paid to give people awful rooms. It's their job.

NANO: Oh, I wish you'd stop being such a Pollyanna all the time.

NICKI: I am not being a Pollyanna—I'm far too much like you.

NANO: Well what's the point of making the best of things all the time if you don't have to?

NICKI: Everybody has to, Nano.

NANO: I don't.

NICKI: Everybody in the world has to but *you*?

NANO: Yep.

NICKI: Well what are you going to do instead?

NANO: Instead of what?

NICKI: Instead of making the best of things—are you just going to get all upset about them? Is that it?

NANO: If I feel like it. If that's what makes me happy—yes. I have that right.
I have that *luxury*.

NICKI: It's going to make you happy to be upset?

NANO: Oh, stop picking me all apart, Nicki. Just because your life isn't the way you want it—well, mine is. Mine is just the way I like it, and when it isn't—I don't have to pretend that it is. I have the right to say I don't like it.

NICKI: *(Suddenly very angry)* GOOD POINT. EXCELLENT POINT. You're absolutely right. I don't know how I could have forgotten that. If the littlest thing doesn't suit you to a T—you just go right ahead, Nano. Get upset.

NANO: *(Also angry)* Thank God your grandfather saw to it that I'd never have to make the best of things, and I'm not about to start now.

NICKI: *(Exploding)* Well maybe I have to, okay? Maybe I have to make the best of things! Maybe I don't have a choice!

(Pause)

NANO: *(She shakes her head, sadly.)* Oh, Nicki...I love our little trips together, but—

NICKI: *(Sits down on the bed next to her)* You know how much I do too—

NANO: I'm getting too old—

NICKI: You are not, don't say that—

NANO: I know we fight sometimes, but—

NICKI: This trip we won't fight.

(Pause)

NANO: Maybe this will be our last trip—maybe you'll find some nice man and get married and the two of you will drive down to Florida together—

NICKI: We'll take you with us—

NANO: Oh, just what a young couple starting out needs—an old hag hanging around—

NICKI: The French do it—it's very European—you always see the French with their grandmother at the beach—

NANO: We do not need to ape the French—we are superior to them in every way—little anti-Semites—yes, they pretend they're not, but you watch, that's where the next Germany will be, you mark my words. If I didn't love my Blue Hour and my Shalimar so much—I just hate myself for buying it, but I can't help myself—

NICKI: *(Laughing)* It's probably made in this country anyhow.

NANO: Is it?

NICKI: Probably.

NANO: I'd feel better—but even if it is, some anti-Semite over there is making money from it.
I bought a couple extra bottles—they run that special every year about now—you want one?

NICKI: No thanks—

NANO: A girl needs to put on a little perfume, Nicki, now please—

NICKI: I said I don't need any—I haven't even started on the bottle you gave me last year.

NANO: No social life at all, Nicki?

NICKI: No… *(She sighs, editing out the social life she can't tell her grandmother about.)* …not the way you mean.

NANO: Well—concentrate. Haven't you learned what the other girls do to get a husband—or don't they get husbands anymore, just bed partners—ooooooooouuuuuuuuch, that's not for you.
Tell me, Nicki—what ever happened to that nice lawyer you were seeing—

NICKI: Is it warm enough for you in here?

NANO: Well, it sure couldn't be any colder.

NICKI: Then you'd rather I didn't open a window?

NANO: OPEN A WINDOW!!! MY GOD, NICKI—IT'S LIKE AN ICE BOX IN HERE!

NICKI: Well then, I guess it's time once again to transform an ordinary Howard Johnson's motel room into the burning depths of hell.

NANO: What do you mean?

NICKI: I'm turning on the heat. Say when... *(She sullenly goes over to the heating unit.)*

(NICKI turns the heat on, to the first setting. There's a loud click.)

NICKI: Mississippi in August?

(NICKI turns it up again. Again, there's a loud click.)

NICKI: Death Valley at high noon?

(NICKI turns it up again, and again, there's a loud click.)

NICKI: Ground zero, Nagasaki, July 1945? *(Pause. She turns the heating setting, but there's no click.)* That will have to do, Nano, that's as high as it goes.

NANO: Nicki, I was like an icicle all day in that car and didn't say a word, but—

NICKI: AN ICICLE—what are you talking about—I had the heat up so high I practically passed out—

NANO: It was freezing in that car—

NICKI: Then how come every time I put on the turn indicator I got a second degree burn—

NANO: After the first few hours I couldn't even feel my toes—

NICKI: I was delirious with heat—

NANO: Right about the time we passed Columbia my legs went numb, but I said—what the hell, maybe I'm having a stroke—

NICKI: *(Dropping the game)* Nano—come on—don't joke—

NANO: *(Still dead serious)* Old people have no business being with the young—

NICKI: I turned it up, Nano, all the way—can you feel it yet?

NANO: Old people deserve what they get—they should never foist themselves on young people for more than short periods at a time, and if they do—well, they get what they deserve, they truly do.

NICKI: *(Changing the subject)* Then who you gonna drive down to Boca with—Pearl Rubenstein? *(She laughs.)* The two of you in your separate cars?

NANO: Well, when we go out we don't want to have an accident— you know the way Pearl talks, we'd be yakking away and the next thing you know, we'd be in a ditch.

NICKI: That must be something to see—the two of you pulling up to the Kentucky Fried Chicken in your matching Fleetwood Broughams.

NANO: No, Pearl's got a new one. White with red leather.

NICKI: That sounds nice.

NANO: She's very particular. Won't even *think* of taking it out in the rain.

NICKI: You really do need a new one—too bad Pearl didn't wait, you could have gotten a deal. Bought your Cadillacs in bulk.

NANO: I don't care what a car looks like, long as it gets me where I'm going. Though it is making a lot of noise lately, they can really hear me coming—surprised you can't hear me all the way in New York.

NICKI: It's nice you have someone to—you know, pal around with.

NANO: Oh, Pearl's all right. She's no good to go shopping with—nothing's good enough. But we do like our fried chicken and she cries on my shoulder about Geraldine, and I cry on hers about you.

NICKI: Gerry's almost five years younger than I am, Nano—

NANO: Yes—you've got a five year head start on her with the men, and look at the good it's done you. Don't you have any social life at all?

(NICKI shrugs.)

NANO: What's wrong with the men—what are they looking for, sex?

NICKI: *(Laughs and shakes her head. This is, after all, what she often looks for in men.)* It'd be a lot easier if they were. Unfortunately most of them are looking for a mother. Or free therapy. But the worst of all—the ones who want to know about you. The relentless cross examination. And not so they can know you and love you, no, no. So they can find out why you're not worth loving. So they can find out what's wrong with you up front. Give me the ones who just want sex, Nano. It's faster, kinder, much more pleasant, and more honest, in the end.

NANO: Sex sex sex—god, what's happening to the world?

(NICKI can't stop laughing.)

NANO: What's so funny?

NICKI: You are.

NANO: Oh, go on. I don't feel funny. I feel very sad.

NICKI: Why?

NANO: I don't know what the future holds for you.

(NANO and NICKI sigh.)

(Lights dim slightly)

Scene Two

(The door into the room opens, and the MAID *enters with her cart.)*

(She is humming My Old Kentucky Home.*)*

*(*NANO *and* NICKI *have gone into the bathroom to change. They seem unaware of the* MAID's *presence, and the* MAID *is unaware of theirs.)*

(The MAID *flips the orange Monets around, and on their reverse side are two orange-tinted Renoirs. She then turns down the beds, and puts a* WELCOME TO PADUCAH, KENTUCKY *sign on the T V.)*

(The door to the hallway is open, and the sound of soda cans being dispensed from a vending machine right next to their room is very loud.)

NANO: *(O S. From the bathroom)* My God, I hope we don't have to listen to that racket all night.

NICKI: *(O S. Also from the bathroom)* I'm sure we won't.

(The cans continue falling.)

NANO: *(O S)* Regular little Miss Mary Sunshine, that's what you are.

NICKI: *(O S)* It's still not too late to change rooms, you know—

NANO: *(O S)* And repack and go traipsing around at this time of night? Not on your life. No telling where we'd end up.

NICKI: *(O S)* Okay. But remember, you had your chance.

NANO: *(O S)* I'll go crazy if this keeps up.

NICKI: *(O S)* You will not.

NANO: *(Entering from the bathroom, wearing her nightgown, robe, and helmet. The* MAID *exits.)* See if I don't.

*(*NANO *gets into bed.* NICKI *enters from the bathroom, wearing a revealing satin and lace nightgown—black. She swirls around as she heads for her bed.)*

NICKI: I really do like this, Nano.

NANO: Well, it's nothing special, but it was a good price.

(The MAID *has closed the door behind her, but the sound of the cans clanging is only slightly muted.)*

NICKI: It's really nice.

NANO: *(As* NICKI *starts to get into bed)* You're not going to wear it tonight, are you?

NICKI: Why not?

NANO: Well, I just thought you were going to save it, that's all.

NICKI: Save it for what, Nano?

NANO: Well, I'm not going to live forever, you know. The way you're going, I won't be around to shop for your trousseau—

NICKI: People do not shop for trousseau anymore, Nano.

NANO: Oh, you know it all, do you?

NICKI: Forget it. *(She turns, heads for the bathroom.)* I'm sorry, I'll take it off, you bought it for me under false pretenses—

NANO: Nicki, please, wear it if you want to—I'm tired and it doesn't matter.

NICKI: I'm sorry. I just—

NANO: I just need a good night's sleep, that's all I need. Though I don't know how I'll get it with that racket going on.

NICKI: I'm gonna go out there with an out of order sign in about two minutes if it keeps up.

NANO: Like that?

NICKI: Yes—sure—why not? Maybe then you'd get your wish—I'd wear this nightgown during acts in keeping with the spirit, if not the letter, of its purchase. *(She drapes herself against the door.)* Yahoo Mountain Dew, Pepsi Caffeine Free, or me.

NANO: I think you're capable of it.

NICKI: Capable of, maybe. Desperate enough, no. Maybe by our trip next year.

NANO: *(Shaking her head)* Oh, Nicki, what are we going to do with you? It's just not right—you have so much to give. Hate to see you go to waste.

NICKI: Yes, it's a real shame.

NANO: A regular tragedy.

NICKI: I wouldn't go that far.

NANO: Maybe what we need to do is mount a campaign, the way Lucille Glitz did for the Felischaker girl back in—I don't know, right after the war, I guess. Lucille had already married off all her girls, and I guess she saw Molly Fleischaker as a real challenge. Well, she set out to get that girl a husband—first she bought her slews of clothes at Hartsfields in Kansas City, that was where you went when you wanted only the very best. Then they went up to Chicago on the train and installed themselves in one of the poshest hotels—can't remember the name, guess my mind is going—and Lucille started giving the parties. She gave 'em all that

season, and by the end of it that Fleischaker girl had
gotten herself a man. From a very nice family, too.

NICKI: Sounds great. When do we leave?

NANO: Oh, I'm too old for that kind of thing. Still, it
was quite an accomplishment for Lucille. She really
knew how to mount a campaign.
Oh, I don't know, Nicki, things were so much easier
back then. I still remember hunting violets with my
boyfriend—must have been all of five years-old. And I
got some tadpoles, that was my first gift from a beau.
(Pause) Well, guess it's time we got some sleep. Night,
dear.

NICKI: (Switching off the light) Night, Nano. Thanks
again for the nightgown.

NANO: You're entirely welcome.

(NANO and NICKI lie in bed, as the soda cans continue to
clang.)

(NICKI swings herself out of bed as quietly as is humanly
possible.)

NANO: Nicki—is something wrong?

NICKI: No, I'm just...going to the bathroom.

NANO: Oh.

(NICKI very quietly takes a pen from her bag and tiptoes into
the bathroom.)

(The light shines out from the bathroom. After a few
moments, NICKI emerges, wearing NANO's coat over her
nightgown—the coat is too short in the sleeves, as well as the
length.)

(NICKI is carrying the paper "FOR YOUR
PROTECTION" strip from the toilet seat. She's written
something on it.)

(NICKI *opens the door to the hall as quietly as she can, and slips out into the hall, after looking both ways to make sure the coast is clear.*)

(*She is halfway out the door when she turns the knob on the door, realizes it will automatically lock after her. She decides to try it anyway—she swings the door open, and holds it with her foot while she leans far to one side, attempting to put the strip of paper on the vending machine.*)

(*All that is visible is her foot in the door. As she inches further and further out of the door to reach the vending machine, the door closes further.*)

NICKI: (*A proud whisper*) Got it! (*But as she attempts to go back into the room, her foot slips, and the door closes the final centimeter. It clicks shut.*)

(*For several seconds, silence*)

(*Then* NICKI *taps quietly on the door.*)

NICKI: Nano? Nano, it's me. Nano? (*Not as loudly, to someone in the hall.*) No, I'm sure I have the right room... no, I will *not* be coming to your room when I have finished... (*Very loud, banging on the door*) NANO!!!!!

NANO: Nicki? (*She switches on the light next to the bed.*) Nicki— (*She sees that* NICKI *is not in bed. She gets up and goes toward the bathroom.*) Nicki, what's wrong—

NICKI: (*O S*) I'm out here, Nano—let me in!
Look, sir, I'm sorry your team lost the big game, but you will have to find another way to make up for it.

NANO: (*She comes out of the bathroom, confused.*) NICKI— where are you?

NICKI: (*O S*) NANO I'M OUT HERE! NANO!!!

NANO: (*Opening the door*) NICKI—what on earth are you doing out here like that?

NICKI: *(She slides inside quick as she can, locking the door behind her. She takes off* NANO's *coat.)* Fixing it so we could get some sleep tonight.

NANO: What do you mean?

NICKI: *(She dashes back to her bed, gets under the covers.)* I put an out of order sign on the coke machine.

NANO: You did *what*?

NICKI: Nano, it's not right that it should keep us up all night. So, I—

NANO: Listen to me, young lady. You go right back out there and take that sign off this minute. I never heard of such a thing.

NICKI: But Nano, you've got to get some sleep.

NANO: If you think I'll be able to sleep a wink now— we don't do this sort of thing, Nicki. If we can't sleep, we don't sleep, but we never, *ever*, stoop to something like this.

NICKI: It's not hurting anybody, Nano, if somebody wants a coke they can just use the machine on another floor.

NANO: That is not the point.

NICKI: I'm not going to take the sign off. There is no reason why we should be bothered all night. And I don't intend to be.

NANO: All right. But I'm getting dressed. I'm going to go sit in the lobby.

NICKI: Nano—

NANO: I will sit up all night in the lobby—

NICKI: None of this would have happened if you'd just let me change our room.

NANO: Why should I always have to be changing rooms all the time? No, Nicki, I won't do it. I paid my money for a room, and if they stick us with rooms like this then they just do it. That's the way it is. I can't be running from room to room all the time—if this is the way it is for travelers today, then I'll just stay at home. Your grandfather and I never had to put up with this kind of—

NICKI: Of course you didn't. He would have gone out there with his shotgun.

NANO: He would not. He was too much of a gentleman.

NICKI: *(Mimes shooting)* Pow. Fountain service.

NANO: That is not the point, Nicki.

NICKI: All right. I'll take the sign off. Give me your coat. *(She takes NANO's coat, puts it back on.)*

NANO: *(Can't help laughing)* Oh, you do look a sight.

NICKI: Hold the door open, would you?

(NANO holds the door while NICKI dashes out.)

NICKI: Look, mister—I don't care how far you drove to see the game, I will not come to your room when I'm through...why not?...because...because...I won't be through. Now let me go—the winning team is waiting in my room. *(She throws herself back into the room.)* Close call. *(She double locks the door.)*

NANO: Who were you talking to?

NICKI: Just a drunk. *(She goes over to her bed, climbs up on it and begins jumping up and down on it, making as much noise as possible.)*

NANO: Nicki—what are you doing! NICKI!! PEOPLE ARE TRYING TO SLEEP!!

NICKI: *(Between grunts and groans)* Got to do it, Nano! It's for our own protection!

NANO: What are you talking about, Nicki—

NICKI: *(Stopping)* Do you think I could make a living as a hooker?

NANO: What?

NICKI: *(She starts up, jumping and groaning again.)* One more really good one ought to do it— *(One really spectacular jump and groan, and she stops.)* The really top of the line prostitutes make thousands of dollars a throw. *(She climbs down off the bed, taking off* NANO's *coat.)* Do you think I could make that much?

NANO: Why? Are you thinking of changing professions?

NICKI: I'd have to invest in a whole new wardrobe, of course.

NANO: Well, anything would be an improvement over your current one. How do you ever expect to land a husband looking like a rag-a-muffin?

NICKI: I'll get a husband who wants a wife who looks like a rag a-muffin, obviously.

NANO: And what good will that do you?

NICKI: For your information, some people like the way I dress. There are some people, some men, for instance, who think I—

(The vending machine starts in again, very loud. They listen for a moment. NANO *sighs.* NICKI *glares at her.)*

*(*NICKI *gets into bed.)*

NANO: I'm sorry, Nicki, I just couldn't let you keep that sign up.

NICKI: I know, Nano. It's all right. Let's just try to get some sleep.

(Very loud can sound again, after she switches off the light.)

NICKI: If we can.

Scene Three

(NANO and NICKI are still lying in bed as the morning light begins to stream through the curtains.)

(The cans continue clanging.)

(NANO and NICKI are lying in the exact same positions they were in at the close of the last scene.)

(NICKI reaches as quietly as possible for her reading glasses, and starts to reach for a magazine.)

NANO: Time to get up yet, Nicki?

NICKI: Guess so. *(She puts the magazine back.)*

NANO: Thought it might be.

NICKI: It didn't keep you up, did it?

NANO: Me? *(Lying)* No.

NICKI: Good.

NANO: Did you get a good night's sleep?

NICKI: Well...

NANO: Oh, Nicki, I'd just hate for you to have to drive if you didn't.

NICKI: *(Also lying)* I slept fine, Nano. Really. You know me.

I was just worried you wouldn't get enough sleep.

NANO: Nicki, you mustn't worry about me. *(She didn't sleep a wink.)* I slept like a log.

NICKI: Good. Well, you want to get into the bathroom first?

NANO: Suppose I should. Hate to get out of my warm bed.

NICKI: Hey, I'll warm it up for you— *(She gets out of bed, and turns on the T V.)* Phil Donahue is on—

NANO: Oh, goody— *(She props herself up in bed.)* Oh, damnit, where are my glasses—

(NICKI comes over to help her look.)

NANO: Damnit, I'm turning into an old woman—

NICKI: Come on, I lose mine all the time—

NANO: I just hate myself for being this way—

NICKI: *(As they tear apart the bed looking)* Nano, it's normal—all normal people loose things—

NANO: *I didn't.* I never did. I always knew exactly where things were—

NICKI: Fine, so before you were perfect, now you've deteriorated to the level of the rest of the human race—

(NANO has become very frantic in her search, NICKI sits down and holds her hands still.)

(NICKI says, slowly:)

NICKI: Now. Let's do this scientifically. You usually keep your glasses right here by the side of the bed, right next to mine— *(She picks up her glasses.)*

—and here are my glasses...so...whose glasses am I wearing...right now...

(NANO puts her hands over her mouth, and rocks with laughter.)

NANO: Oh, Nicki— *(She claps.)* I don't believe it—

NICKI: *(Taking off NANO's glasses, handing them to her, putting on her own.)* Oh my god.

NANO: I don't feel so bad now.

NICKI: Wow—one night without sleep and bingo—I've got the eyes of an eighty-four year old.

NANO: You too?

(NICKI nods, they laugh again.)

NANO: What a picture—the two of us lying here quiet as mice, trying not to wake the-other one up—

NICKI: I guess I should have gotten us another room.

NANO: Too much trouble. We'll survive.

(NICKI *has gone over to the T V.*)

NICKI: Loud enough for you?

NANO: Maybe a little louder.

(NICKI turns it up, and heads for the bathroom.

(*The clanging of the cans is muted somewhat while the T V is on.*)

(*On the* Donahue *show, a survivalist is being interviewed. Snippets of her pessimistic harangue are heard.*)

(NICKI *has turned on the hot water in the shower, and stands just visible in the doorway, fanning the steam into the rest of the room with a large bath towel.*)

VOICE OF SURVIVALIST: Water rationing in major cities and most of the south will be common place by the year 2000. There will be strict penalties for breaking the once a week only bathing law.

NANO: Oooouuuh—Thank god I'll be dead by then.

NICKI: (*Can't hear*) What?

NANO: (*Yelling*) They say the water shortage is going to get so bad, they're only going to let us take a bath *once a week*. I'd rather be dead. (*In order to hear better, she has moved to the foot of the bed, taking the covers, wrapping herself in a cocoon. She is able to turn the T V up and down, to facilitate talking to* NICKI.)

NICKI: When did they say this was going to happen?

NANO: Just fifteen or twenty years from now.

NICKI: (*Does a quick computation*) Okay—it's a deal.

NANO: What is?

NICKI: In fifteen years you'll be ninety-nine years old. No one's going to complain if you die then.

NANO: *(Horrified)* Fifteen more years—*why*—what for!

NICKI: Your mother lived to be eighty-seven.

NANO: So?

NICKI: And Aunt Mary to ninety-five.

NANO: Yes, well Aunt Mary had a lot of heartbreak in her life.

NICKI: *(Stops fanning for a moment)* What has that got to do with it?

NANO: Aunt Mary was just hanging on from the start— her husband and her babies died when she was just a young girl and she had to hang on then, we all forced her to—when she got to be an old woman she didn't have the sense to stop, she just kept hanging on, like it was the only thing she knew how to do.

NICKI: Nano—that doesn't make any sense. *(She starts fanning again.)*

NANO: *(Under her breath, almost viciously.)* Oh what do you know about it.

NICKI: What?

NANO: Shush, I want to listen.

VOICE OF SURVIVALIST: Meat will become a rare, precious luxury as more and more grazing land is put into crops grown for direct human consumption.

NANO: No one but the rich will be able to afford hamburger—

NICKI: What—

NANO: *(Yelling)* Only people lousy with money will be able to eat meat—

NICKI: That's okay, we eat too much anyway. Not good for you.

NANO: I like a good hamburger.

NICKI: Hey, you remember that Safeway commercial they ran with you leaning over into the meat compartment?

NANO: That was not me.

NICKI: Sure was. You were the only person in town that year who could afford to buy a piece of steak.

NANO: Well Pearl and I go to the Sizzlin' two or three times a week. Their number 13 Trailhand Burger costs us a dollar sixty-nine and we think we're eating like royalty.

VOICE OF SURVIVALIST: People will marry later, wait longer to have and have fewer children. As the work force grows grayer, and automation continues to...

NICKI: *(She has turned off the shower, and comes back into the bedroom.)* There, that should warm you up some. What are they talking about now?

NANO: Oh, turn it off. I'm sick of listening to these self styled voices of doom.

(NICKI turns it off.)

NANO: Every time I turn on Donahue nowadays, it's people wanting approval for sleeping with people they're not married to, or people who think the government owes them a living, or people talking about why they beat their children—imagine, hitting little babies just because things didn't go your way at work. What's wrong with people? Why can't they just be happy? I don't think happiness is so terrible, do you?

NICKI: *(Quietly)* No.

NANO: Well it isn't. My God, these women on welfare, having slews and slews of babies—they don't even know who the fathers are—I'd sterilize 'em all—

NICKI: Come on, Nano, you don't know what it's like for them—

NANO: The hell I don't. I went through a depression.

NICKI: So? You never had to worry about what you were gonna eat. You never had to worry that you wouldn't be able to feed your baby.

NANO: Well I certainly didn't go out and have another just because I didn't know how to feed the first.

NICKI: When you've got a little baby, Nano, you've got somebody to love that loves you back. These women don't have anything else, so they just keep having babies—it's not their fault, they just—

NANO: Breeding like animals. Proud, yes, proud of the fact that every damn one of their litter has a different father. I'd let the women have two, yes, let 'em have two children and then I'd sterilize 'em—the men I'd castrate right off the bat.

NICKI: I can't stand it when you get like this—I can't— you've got to realize—you don't know what it's like for those people—

NANO: I went through a depression—don't tell me I don't know what it's like—I wanted more than one child, it would have been easy for me to just keep having and having but I had a responsibility—

NICKI: You can't seriously believe there's any comparison between what you went through in the depression, and—

NANO: Your grandfather lost *seven stores*, Nicki. All *seven stores*, that he had worked from nothing to build up, gone overnight, like that.

The banks took everything. And he had to turn right around and start over from scratch. Nobody ever gave him anything. He had to work hard for what he got.

NICKI: I know that but it's different now. You want these people to live by your rules, but you don't know the first thing about what it's like for them.

NANO: Is that so. Well who are you to tell me different? When did you ever worry about a roof over your head? When did you ever not have enough to eat? You've just had it too soft, that's all—you've had it so soft you think you can afford to give it away—it's my tax money that pays to feed all those poor little babies, it's my money they give so all those women can lie down with any man that happens by—

NICKI: *(Yelling)* It's not like that, Nano.

NANO: *(Very firmly)* Don't you tell me what it is or isn't. I have not lived eighty-four years to be told I don't know a thing.

NICKI: *(Restrained)* The bathroom should be warm enough now.

NANO: In a way I'm glad I'm old. *(She gets off her bed.)* Yes. In a way I'm kind of *delighted*.

(Lights dim slightly as NANO *and* NICKI *go into the bathroom.)*

Scene Four

(The MAID *enters with her cart.)*

(She is humming Tennessee Waltz and smoking a cigarette.)

(She makes up the beds, flipping the bedspreads over to their color coordinated other side.)

*(*NANO *and* NICKI *are in the bathroom.)*

NANO: *(O S)* Well, what's on the agenda today?

NICKI: *(O S)* Thought we'd stop in at that Factory Outlet Mall we've been seeing the signs for.

NANO: *(O S)* Oh, I don't know, Nicki, those places, bunch of junk.

NICKI: *(O S)* You never know. We might score some Really Big Bargains.

(The sounds of water running, the toilet flushing, etc.)

NANO: *(O S)* Stop being so damn optimistic all the time. Honestly, Nicki, it takes so little to please you sometimes I wonder. I remember the time you got all these nice presents for your birthday, you were just a little bit of a thing, and... *(She sniffs loudly.)* Nicki—do you smell smoke?

NICKI: *(O S. Sniffing loudly)* No, I...well, yes, a little —

NANO: *(O S)* Well let's hurry up and get out of here—

NICKI: *(O S)* It's probably just someone smoking in the hallway or something.

NANO: *(O S)* Sure hope that's all it is. I'd hate to have to go running out of here in my slip.
Well, anyway, you'd gotten all these presents—some sweet little dresses, new patent leather shoes, all kinds of things, but they weren't what you wanted. No, you wanted toys. Well, some way or other we'd all forgotten to get you any. You were about five, I guess. You started screaming. Couldn't quiet you down. Your grandfather had to take off and run to the five and dime, that was all that was open, and buy you some piddling little balloons. Well, I'd never seen such a—

NANO & NICKI *(O S)* —transformation.

NICKI: *(Enters from the bathroom, zipping up her skirt)* The signs say it's just off the highway, won't be out of our way.

NANO: *(Joining* NICKI *at the door, also dressed and ready to go.)* Oh, all right. Might be fun. You're a shopper, Nicki, I'll say that for you. Can't get your mother to go shopping with me to save my soul.

*(*NICKI *opens the door.)*

NANO: What have they got at this mall—handbags— clothing— *(She looks at* NICKI'*s sandals.)* Maybe you can pick up some nice *shoes.*

NICKI: *(They go into the hallway.)* Only if they're really reduced.

NANO: *(The door swings shut behind them.)* All right, but don't go talking me into buying things for myself I don't really need. I don't believe in spending money just to be spending it.

(The MAID *puts the finishing touches on the room.)*

(She then places a NASHVILLE WELCOMES YOU TO THE COUNTRY MUSIC CAPITOL OF THE WORLD *sign on the T V.)*

(She goes to the door, takes a final long puff of her cigarette, and opens the door. She attempts to push her cart out into the hall.)

(She runs into NANO *and* NICKI *as they come bursting into the room, each loaded down with shopping bags marked* DANSK FACTORY OUTLET. *Nicki mutters "Excuse me" etc., to the* MAID. *The* MAID *does not reply.)*

(After a very brief slapstick moment of jostling, the MAID *is able to gain the hallway. She closes the door behind her.)*

NANO: *(She stumbles to the bed)* Help me, Nicki, I'm going down—

*(*NICKI *drops her bags on the bed and then takes* NANO'*s from her.* NANO *plops down on the bed.)*

NANO: *Look* at it all—how will we ever get it all in the car?

NICKI: There's plenty of room.

NANO: I wish I'd bought that china.

NICKI: We can still go back.

NANO: Now let's see—the dinner plates were originally fifteen dollars a piece—

NICKI: Half off, then half of that, then an additional twenty five percent off that—

NANO: My god, they were practically giving it away! How could you let me get out of there without that china! I could just shoot myself.

NICKI: Well, we did get a lot of other stuff...

NANO: Yes, my casseroles—I'm crazy about my casseroles—let's look at 'em—

(NICKI *finds three large red casseroles in a bag.*)

NANO: —let's see—they were forty-five and sixty dollars a piece—what did we get 'em for?

NICKI: About ten each for these—twelve for the big one—

NANO: Oh, I could just shoot myself about that china. If your grandfather were still alive, I would have picked it up in a minute.

NICKI: What has that got to do with it, Nano, the dishes you're using now are nothing but nicks and cracks.

NANO: Well, so they look terrible, I know they do. Nobody but me uses them. I could just kick myself for not getting it—you or your sister could always have used it after I'm gone.

NICKI: I wish you wouldn't talk like that.

NANO: It was nice china, Nicki, but it certainly wasn't the kind of thing you worry about taking with you to the grave.

(NICKI *pulls two huge wooden salad bowls out of a bag.*)

NANO: How many of those did we get?

NICKI: Two or three, I think—now where's the third...

NANO: Looks like we've got the whole store here. Oh, I don't know what came over me—I haven't done any real entertaining since your grandfather died-

NICKI: *(Taking out a large glass vase)* I just love this—

NANO: We get more than the one?

NICKI: No, you were afraid it would break in the car.

NANO: You take it then—

NICKI: But we only got it because you liked it so well—

NANO: You take it back with you to New York. You'll get much more use out of it than I will.

NICKI: Well—okay. But—

NANO: What else have we got?

NICKI: Well, a couple of these— *(Bright plastic trivets in the shape of a fish)* —and three of these, they were so cheap— *(Red plastic colanders)* —and you got two sauce pans with wooden handles— *(Hunts to find them)*

NANO: Yes, I did need those—but I could have made do with just one—

NICKI: Come on, Nano, I had to stop you from buying three more—

NANO: Well I don't know what I was thinking, then. Temporary insanity. I'm an old woman, Nicki—I don't even cook for myself anymore. It's not worth all the fuss and bother. I wish I hadn't gotten all this stuff.

NICKI: You're tired—that's all it is—we shopped too long—

NANO: What have I got to be tired about—all I've done is sit in a car all day and look at the scenery—such as it is.

NICKI: You'll feel different when we get it all home, you will—

NANO: Oh, let me be. What's there to be excited about in a couple of pots and pans. Cooking's work—hard, hard work, and I'm tired of it. Tired of it all, and I have a right to be.

NICKI: Okay, okay—let's just take it all back— *(She angrily starts throwing everything back into the bags.)* —after all, we only spent three hours shopping for it. What does that matter—it was all just a terrible mistake—you want three red casseroles, but we can only find two, that's all right, let's get the manager, let her hunt one up, that's all right, it's her job. She had no way of knowing you didn't really want it, it was all some kind of joke, it was just a little game you like to play— *(She begins to cry.)* Let's just take it all back. All of it...every bit of it back...

NANO: What are you crying about, Nicki—

NICKI: It's not fair, Nano—it's not. You were having such a good time shopping for all this, it was all going so well, and then we get back and just like that it's all wrong—it's just not fair.

NANO: Good Lord, do I have to walk on egg-shells with you? Can't I say what's on my mind?

NICKI: Yes, yes, of course.

NANO: Honestly, Nick, I'm eighty-four years old—you can't expect me to just keep on and on and on—

NICKI: Why not—why can't I!

NANO: Because you can't.

NANO: I should never have attempted this trip. It's too hard on you, you try so hard to please me, and—

NICKI: I do—I do try—

NANO: I know you do. I just shouldn't have attempted it. I just can't do it anymore.

NICKI: That's right—that's right—say it—go ahead and say what you know will hurt me the most—tell me you're sorry you came with me—sorry you took the time out of your busy schedule.

NANO: I like my life, Nicki—why shouldn't I like my life? My own house, my own schedule, the way I like to do things, the things I like to eat—why should you be hurt because I like my life?

NICKI: You always do this to me—you always do—

NANO: Oh, Nicki, come on, let's stop this, I'm just tired. You know I don't know what I'm doing when I'm tired.

NICKI: I know—I'm sorry I kept you shopping so long—

NANO: You kept me? Wild horses couldn't of dragged me away from those bargains.

(NICKI *goes to* NANO, *they hold each other.*)

NANO: There.

You think I don't know where I'd be without you, Nicki? You children are all I've got—but sometimes I don't like to be reminded of that, that's all.

Now, let's look at the rest of our purchases.

(NICKI *pulls a bizarre kitchen gadget from one of the bags— it is a cross between a grater, a fly swatter, and a garlic press. She hands it to* NANO.)

NANO: This looks interesting.

NICKI: Yes, I thought so too. What are you going to do with it?

NANO: Me? I thought you wanted it—

NICKI: It was in the shopping cart, I thought you put it there—

NANO: Me? What on earth would I do with it?

(NANO and NICKI inspect the gadget carefully.)

NICKI: I have no idea. Let's see—it was originally seven-fifty—

NANO: And we paid all of thirty-five cents for it! *(She holds it up to the light.)* Well, I have no idea what to do with it, but it's certainly a bargain.

NICKI: I think I finally got us a decent room. We're right over the swimming pool— *(She goes over to the sliding glass doors, opens them.)* —you'd have to be nuts to swim in weather like this.

(Loud thuddering noise as someone vaults off the diving board, followed by a tremendous splash.)

NANO: Wouldn't put it past some of 'em. Bunch of lunatics.

NICKI: Well, the sign says the pool closes at nine, so it won't be too bad. *(She bends over the railing, squinting.)* Oh, no.

NANO: Put on a sweater if you're going to stay out there long.

NICKI: *(Under her breath)* Happy...Birthday...Betty... *(Closes the door, goes over to the heating unit. Nervously)* You warm enough?

NANO: What's wrong—doesn't that thing work?

NICKI: Yes, of course it works. *(It's not working.)* I'm just adjusting it. *(It's still not working.)* Of course, if you're warm enough, I won't bother.

Are you warm enough?

NANO: Oh, don't ask me. I'm half dead and I don't know.

NICKI: *(She turns all the knobs one last time, then gives the heating unit a good swift kick. The heat comes on.)* There we go. You should be warmed up in no time.

NANO: *(Wearily)* If you say so, Nicki.

NICKI: *(As she moves away from the sliding glass doors, the very loud sound of an electric guitar being tuned)* Oh, no.

NANO: What was that—

NICKI: *(Guilty, she's failed again.)* This wonderful room... is right over...what seems to be a patio party...HAPPY BIRTHDAY BETTY FROM ALL THE GANG AT WORK.

NANO: Oh, jimminy...

NICKI: Two guitars, drums of course, saxophone, stand up bass—

(The guitar sound is tripled, booming into the room.)

NICKI: —and I believe they've just finished hooking up all four seven foot amps.

NANO: Let's go out, go eat dinner, maybe they'll blow a fuse by the time we get back.

NICKI: Where do you want to go?

NANO: Let's find some place different—I'm kinda sick of eating at Howard Johnson's every night.

NICKI: Fine with me. What do you feel like?

NANO: Any place you want to go, long as it's not too swish. Though I think it should be some place near— I'd kinda hate to pile back in the car, wouldn't you?

NICKI: I wouldn't mind, but if you do, then—

NANO: It would be fun to explore, but I don't know, I'm kinda beat.

NICKI: Well, we could always walk a block or two and see what's what—

NANO: Oh, it's too cold out for that, don't you think—

NICKI: Well, we could always eat downstairs—

NANO: I'm sick of their food, aren't you?

NICKI: Yes, but if you're too tired to go out—

NANO: I really am, Nicki. I just hate to make you eat at Howard Johnson's again.

NICKI: Nano I don't mind. Really—

NANO: And I know you must be tired from all the driving—

NICKI: I am not. I like driving. I'm a good driver.

NANO: Yes, you certainly are. I always feel so safe when I'm in the car with you.

NICKI: I wish you'd wear your seat belt—it makes me mad you won't.

NANO: Damn awful things, creep up on you, like to strangle you.

NICKI: I'd feel a lot better if you did.

NANO: Can't breathe when I've got one of those damn things on. No, I'm living too long anyway.

NICKI: NANO!

NANO: Oh, all right.
I do admire you modern girls, though. If something were to happen to us on the road, you'd be able to cope with it. Now if I were alone and got a flat tire—I might as well just stretch myself out across the highway and pray for somebody to run over me.

NICKI: *(Laughing)* Come on, Nano, that's not true.

NANO: It is. A car is a great mystery to me. I can drive it, and that's about it.
I'd just as soon eat here, if it's all right with you.

NICKI: It's fine. You know I don't care where we eat. Quantity, not quality, that's my moto.

NANO: In my day, people appreciated good food. Of course, you worked harder for it back then. You didn't have lovely big grocery stores, with all kinds of convenience foods the way you do now. The women slaved over the meals, and when you sat down, you knew you were sitting down to something wonderful. I don't know what's wrong with people today. They go out to eat, throw money away on slop, but they act like a big, beautiful family dinner is the worst thing that could happen to them. They don't eat this, they don't eat that. And the way your sister is bringing up those two children of her—well, she's practically starving those two little babies.

NICKI: She is not.

NANO: All I said to them was that they could have some ice cream if they cleaned their plates. What was wrong with that? It's good for children to eat. But your sister screamed at me. She said "Don't you dare bribe them to eat. I don't want them to eat like that." She yelled at me, Nicki. So I didn't do it anymore.

NICKI: She didn't mean to, Nano, I'm sure she just meant—

NANO: (*Completely defeated*) Imagine someone not wanting their children to like to eat.

NICKI: We'd better go on down, Nano. Before they close—

NANO: I'm living in a dream world...

NICKI: You are not. Now come on—

NANO: You're sure it's all right with you—

NICKI: You know it is.

NANO: *(More brightly)* You know me, a hamburger is just what I like. But you get yourself a steak or something.

NICKI: Nano, no one orders steak at Howard Johnson's.

(As NANO and NICKI head for the door, the loud rock music begins to real. They yell over it.)

NANO: Why not?

NICKI: They're not any good.

NANO: They're not? Then let's go some place where they are.

NICKI: *(As they exit)* Nano, I don't want a steak.

NANO: Why not? Your mother and father love a nice steak.

(The door shuts behind them, as the rock music increases.)

(Lights dim slightly)

Scene Five

(The loud rock music continues playing.)

(The door opens, very slowly. NANO and NICKI enter the room. NANO is leaning on NICKI, and they are taking it a step at a time.)

(The rock music comes to a crescendo, then stops. Applause filters in, then there is relative silence.)

(NICKI helps NANO over to the bed.)

NANO: It's freeeeezing in here. They haven't got the air conditioning on, have they? It's like an ice box in here.

NICKI: *(Goes over to the heating/air conditioning unit, begins fiddling with the controls.)* No, it's not.

(NICKI *gives the unit another good swift kick. The heat comes on.)*

NANO: Have people gone crazy? Have they lost their minds? All this talk about the energy crisis—here I've been suffering through the winters, keeping my thermostat way down, and—

NICKI: The air conditioning is off, Nano.

NANO: Well see that it stays off.

NICKI: Are you feeling any better?

NANO: I don't know. My dinner just didn't sit well with me.

NICKI: It's all that fried food. All you ever eat is fried food.

NANO: Oh, stop it, Nicki. I know what I like to eat. *(She sighs.)* I don't know, Nicki. Everything's so changed. Not at all the way I remember it. Why when your grandfather and I used to drive down every winter— Nicki, do you think we could go through Daytona Beach?

NICKI: Sure—if you want to.

NANO: I'd kinda like to. Haven't been there since your grandfather and I took that last trip. That was the year we drove down with the Rubensteins—Pearl and Roger. Well, you know, Daytona Beach in those days was restricted.

NICKI: Daytona Beach? Why?

NANO: In those days it was quite posh. Well, we had our reservations, but when we walked in with the Rubensteins, they were suddenly full up. I remember distinctly that the man at the desk had the guts to suggest that he would call up one of the unrestricted hotels and get us a room there. Well your grandfather raised the roof. "I most certainly will not let you do that" he said. Roger Rubenstein was such a gentleman, he just kept saying quietly, "We have a confirmed reservation". But your grandfather raised the roof. So then—then the man had the nerve to suggest that we go to the restricted hotel next door, and register under an assumed name! Well, that got me really mad, I was boiling, I told him "I have *never* needed to use a name other than my own. I have nothing to apologize for!" Roger Rubenstein was such a gentleman—he never raised his voice. But your grandfather—not your grandfather. Nobody ever pushed your grandfather around.

Oh, I'll never forget it. You see, it turned out that they really were full—and so we had to wait till the bar was closed, and the dancing was done, and they wheeled four cots into the lounge and set them up, side by side, and that's where the four of us slept—me, your grandfather, Roger, and Pearl. Poor Pearl—she wasn't even really Jewish, and they still didn't want her.

Oh, I'll never forget it—Pearl and I were draped over those big chairs in the lobby waiting to go to bed, we were dead, and a couple of drunks came out of the bar and said "Hiya, toots". *(She laughs softly, remembering. Pause)* It was lovely down there, then, prejudice and all. There's no prejudice here now, I suppose—no room for it.

Oh, you should have seen the four of us, sleeping together, a regular dormitory. We slept in our clothes—Pearl in her slip, she was such a clothes horse, didn't want to get her nice dress all wrinkled. Oh, but I was mad when he suggested that we register somewhere under an assumed name.

NICKI: And that was the last trip you took.

NANO: Yes, the very last. He died the day after we got home. *(Softly)* Oceans and oceans.

NICKI: What?

NANO: Oceans and oceans. Of you know, love. That's what he put on the card with that butter-suede jacket, I'd seen it in a shop but I refused, I refused to buy it, why it was an outrage, charging that much for a little jacket you couldn't even wear in the rain, but I did love it, and the last day we were in Miama, he'd slipped out while I was in the beauty shop, and bought it and hid it in the Rubenstein's luggage. Roger gave it to me at the funeral.

He shouldn't have done that. He should have waited. I almost lost my mind when I opened that box. But he didn't know any better. If it had been Pearl, you see, she would have wanted that new jacket on her back immediately, nothing in the world could have made her feel better, but I wasn't like Pearl. I saw it in the box, and I read that card, and I thought I would just die.

NICKI: Do you remember the name of the hotel? Where they didn't want to let you stay?

(NANO *goes into the bathroom to change.*)

NANO: *(O S)* In Daytona Beach? My Lord, no Nicki, it was almost twenty years ago.

NICKI: Well, would you remember it if you saw it? We could stay there now if we can find it—

NANO: *(O S)* Whatever for? Oh, no, Nicki, let's not bother with Daytona Beach—it was going downhill even when your grandfather and I were there. Let's just keep on driving, and—

NICKI: You don't want to go to Daytona Beach?

NANO: *(O S)* Not really, no.

NICKI: A minute ago you did.

NANO: *(O S)* So? I didn't know what I was saying. I thought about it and I changed my mind.

NICKI: Okay with me, it's just a minute ago you really wanted to go.

NANO: *(O S)* Nicki, if you want to go, then of course we will—

NICKI: NANO. I don't want to go. We were just going to go because you wanted to.

NANO: *(O S)* Well I don't want to.

NICKI: Yeah. I know.

NANO: *(O S)* I'd much rather we just kept on driving, and then one day next week maybe drive down to Miama Beach just for fun, just to see what it looks like down there.

NICKI: I guess we could. But it's kind of dangerous there now.

NANO: *(O S)* Miama Beach?

NICKI: I don't know about Miami Beach, but Miami is the drug capitol of the world.

NANO: *(O S)* I can't believe that—you must be mistaken.

NICKI: Couple years from now nobody's gonna be safe south of Lauderdale.

NANO: *(She comes out of the bathroom, ready for bed.)* It can't be true—why in my day it was so elegant— every night the people would go out, almost like a promenade, you'd go from hotel to hotel visiting. Sidewalks so crowded with all the women in their hats. And the food—oh, my, the food you got back then. Nothing at all like the slop we had tonight.

NICKI: We could drive down if you wanted to, but really— nothing there but a lot of real old people holed up in their condos and drug runners...God, if you could just get them working together—

NANO: On Collins Avenue it was a regular parade—
Mamma had so many friends, it would take us all night
just to say hello to them—

NICKI: It'd be great—they'd never check you—we
could bring back pounds of it—I'd plant it on you
without telling you, and—

NANO: I'd like to see you try.

NICKI: Think of all the money we could make—

NANO: Yes, and spend the rest of my life in some
prison?

NICKI: Prison's where you get the really good drugs—
that and elementary schools, the very best.

NANO: Don't joke about it. It's not funny.

NICKI: *(Hiding the truth by telling it)* Who's joking? *(Then
quickly covers up)* Do you feel like watching a little T V,
or do you want to go straight to sleep?

NANO: There's nothing good on anymore. Just as soon
go to sleep.

NICKI: Might as well. Nothing to do around here.

(Rock music begins again.)

NICKI: Nano, would you mind if—

NANO: If what?

NICKI: If I went downstairs for a few minutes.

NANO: Do you want to get a paper or something?
That wouldn't be bad at all. See what's going on in the
world.

NICKI: Okay, sure. I'll get you a paper. *(She takes her
purse and heads for the door.)* I won't be gone—

NANO: You won't be gone long, will you?

NICKI: No, not too long.

(The music from the party begins throbbing into the room again.)

NANO: Don't be too long.

NICKI: I won't.

(NICKI leaves. NANO double locks the door behind her.)

(NANO picks up her purse, and goes over to the chairs near the sliding glass door. She sits down in one of them, her purse in her lap.)

(The music continues blaring into the room.)

(To indicate time lapse of 20 or 30 minutes, rock music plays 3 or 4 bars each of 5 or 6 songs appropriate to a mediocre "cover" band.)

(NANO, who has been sitting perfectly still, gets up from the chair. She goes into the bathroom, brings out her clothing. She lays her suit on the bed. She takes off her robe, but not her nightgown. She puts on her suit over her nightgown, hiking it up so that it won't show. She puts on her hose, rolling them above the knee, but not her girdle. She takes off her helmet, puts on her shoes, and sits down on her bed near the phone. She pulls the phone a few inches closer, puts her purse near her feet, checks her watch once, and waits.)

(The band plays another set of fragments, then breaks. NANO looks at her watch again, and reaches for the phone.)

NICKI: *(The sound of a key in the door—the door opens a few inches, but is stopped by the chain.)* Nano? Nano why'd you lock the door—

NANO: *(She jumps up from the bed and runs over to open the door.)* NICKI—is that you—I've been worried sick—

NICKI: Worried? Why would you be worried, Nano—

(NANO unchains the door, NICKI comes in and double locks the door behind her.)

NICKI: I was just downstairs.

NANO: I was just about to call the police.

NICKI: The police—

NANO: Well, I was sitting here trying to think who I should call when you didn't come back. I'd call George first, to come and get me and drive the car back home—

NICKI: Nano, I've only been gone about an hour—

NANO: I've just been sitting here picturing all the terrible things that could have happened to you. For all I knew you were lying in a ditch somewhere.

NICKI: How would I have gotten to this ditch from the lobby of the motel?

NANO: Someone would have hit you over the head and dragged you there.

NICKI: That's ridiculous.

NANO: And then I'd be stuck here alone and I wouldn't know what to do. So I was making a list in my head of who I should call first.

NICKI: Nano, if I were lying in a ditch the first person you should call is mom and dad.

NANO: Oh, I wouldn't call your mother on a bet.

NICKI: Why not?

NANO: Wouldn't want to disturb her.

NICKI: NANO IF I AM LYING WITH MY HEAD BASHED IN IN A DITCH DISTURBING MOTHER IS THE LEAST OF YOUR PROBLEMS.

NANO: Oh, a lot you know about it. *(She begins taking off her suit, getting her robe back on, etc.)*

NICKI: Look, I'm sorry you were worried—there was a band playing, and I guess I just lost track of time—

NANO: You did not say anything to me about going to hear some band play. If you want to go listen to bands, it's fine with me, but not while I am with you, waiting alone in some motel room, imagining the most horrible things.

NICKI: I would have called/but I—

NANO: /You had no business—

NICKI: I didn't want to wake you up, /you were so—

NANO: /If you think I could go to sleep while you were God knows where—

NICKI: *Okay*, Nano, *all right.* I said I WAS SORRY. I won't do it again.

NANO: See that you don't.

(NANO *is dressed for bed, and starts to climb in.*)

NICKI: *Okay.*

(NICKI *begins undressing, goes into the bathroom.*)

NANO: *(Getting out of bed, looking around)* Have you got the paper in there with you?

NICKI: What?

NANO: The paper. *(Still looking)*

NICKI: *(O S)* Oh, no... *(She comes back in, pulling her skirt on.)* I'll be right back, Nano—

NANO: You didn't get one?

NICKI: I forgot—

NANO: Well just forget it then.

NICKI: It will take me all of two seconds—

NANO: If you think I'm going to go through this all over again you've got another think coming.

NICKI: But—

NANO: I'll do without.

NICKI: *(Throws up her hands, goes back to the bathroom.)* All right. Okay. Okay.

NANO: I'll be glad when this trip is over.

(NICKI comes back, folds her arms. Glares)

NICKI: Nano. Why do you say things like that? You do it on purpose, right? Just to upset me. You know I can't stand it when you—

NANO: We like different things, Nicki. Why should two people who like to do different things go on trips together and made each other miserable?

NICKI: But we don't—

NANO: If I gave you the money, you could take it and go someplace nice instead of going on these trips with me.

NICKI: I said I was sorry.

NANO: That would make a lot more sense.

NICKI: Why?

NANO: These trips are expensive, Nicki. You could have a week in one of those fancy resorts for what it costs.

NICKI: With the young boy of my choice? You're on.

NANO: I meant by yourself.

NICKI: We'll go to Acalpoco. I'll teach him everything I know.

NANO: And what would that be?

NICKI: Uh...the stock market?

NANO: Oh, of course.

NICKI: Really, Nano, if I can't take a young boy I'd just as soon take you.

NANO: Thank you very much, I'm very flattered.

NICKI: You're welcome.

NANO: No, what you need is somebody established—somebody of substance. It wouldn't kill you to take a look at a man who's really made something of himself, now would it?

NICKI: I've taken a look all right. And they all make me feel like I'm out with my father. Except he'd be more fun.

NANO: Now that nice lawyer you were seeing—

NICKI: You remember how you used to tell us the most important rule of marriage? Marry a man taller than you, so you can gain all the weight you want and still look small when you walk with him into a room?

NANO: He sounded so nice, the way you described him on the phone.

NICKI: Well, I was set for life, I mean he was like six foot four, but it turned out we couldn't stand each other.

NANO: Why, what was wrong with him?

NICKI: He lied to me.

NANO: About what?

NICKI: His height.

NANO: Well it must have been something, Nicki. He came from a very nice family, you said, and he had a lovely position, and—

NICKI: If you really want to know, Nano—

NANO: WELL OF COURSE I DO.

NICKI: I couldn't...I didn't like it when he...you know...when...I mean, you have to be attracted to them don't you?

NANO: Oh. I see.

NICKI: You have to at least think they're nice to have around, right?

NANO: You can't marry someone that repulses you. That would be a terrible mistake.

NICKI: Right.

NANO: Was there something...really wrong with him?

NICKI: You mean, was he missing anything? No, it was all there. It's just that...you remember what Uncle Joseph looked like with all that hair growing out of his ears?

NANO: He looked like Uncle Joseph! Well no wonder!

NICKI: Of course he didn't, Nano. He was just...very nice, but not my type.

NANO: I'd say you were getting a little old to be so particular.

NICKI: That's what got me into trouble in the first place. I said to myself "Don't be so particular. This is a nice guy, right? Isn't nice more important than, say, fashion sense? Isn't nice more important than... table manners? Isn't nice more important than the fact that his brief case has more sex appeal than the rest of him put together? This is a nice guy. Go out with him. Keep going out with him. So what if going on a date with him feels like going to the chair."

NANO: That bad?

NICKI: Okay, I'm exaggerating a little. But it didn't matter how nice a guy Uncle Joseph was, did it? No, it did not make his ear hair go away. And it didn't matter how hard I tried to fall in love with the lawyer. No matter how hard I tried to see him as the man of my dreams, this...boring adult in a pinstriped suit was still there.

NANO: You're well out of it then, Nicki. I wouldn't have you in an unhappy marriage for anything in the world.

NICKI: Right.

NANO: And if the Jewish men are just too dumb to appreciate you—you go right ahead and marry a gentile.

NICKI: You don't mean that. Oh sure, you can say it now, because it's safe. I haven't just waltzed in the door with Henrich Von Schmitd the third on my army— but if I did, oh boy. When people asked about me you'd say "Nicki? Nicki who?"

NANO: *(Angry)* Maybe your mother and father would try and stop you, but I wouldn't. No, I've seen what it is for a woman to be alone.

NICKI: Come on, Nano. What about the time Davey Rubenstein married that little Baptist girl from Arkansas and you didn't even want to send a wedding present.

NANO: That was entirely different.

NICKI: It's the same thing.

NANO: Why should you be alone because those stinkers are chasing after blondes? Well, let 'em have 'em, that's what I say. I hope they all get divorced and their wives bleed 'em for every dime they've got. Serve 'em right. But you get yourself some happiness in your life.

NICKI: It's really all right with you if he's not Jewish?

NANO: Absolutely.

NICKI: Well, it does open up the field a bit.
You really mean it?

NANO: As long as he loves you, and you love him, that's all that matters.

NICKI: What if he's black?

NANO: Nicki!

NICKI: But you just said—

NANO: I know what I just said.

NICKI: What if he were Jewish. The Ethiopian Jews are black. You couldn't say a word if I brought an Ethiopian Jew home.

NANO: We've got to get you married—and soon—before it's too late.

NICKI: Too late for what?

NANO: You know exactly what I mean, young lady.

NICKI: Oh.

NANO: Instead of wasting your vacation on me—

NICKI: Here we go again...

NANO: Maybe you go to one of those places where young people go, Club Med I think they call them—

NICKI: Nano— *(Condescending tone)* Do you know what those places *are*?

NANO: Yes—they're places where young people go to meet each other. Pearl told me Geraldine was thinking of going to one off the coast of Spain—

NICKI: You're kidding.

NANO: No. Why would I be kidding? Geraldine makes a nice salary, not as good as yours, of course, she's no genius, but—

NICKI: Geraldine wouldn't last two seconds at one of those places.

NANO: Why?

NICKI: Because she's...fat.

NANO: She is not—she's a very pretty girl.

NICKI: If she was all that pretty, Nano, she wouldn't have to go to Club Med to get...to have...Nano, those places are for people to go and sleep with each other.

NANO: Oh, no, Nicki, you're wrong.

NICKI: You know what those places are like? The minute you get there they take all your money and give you strings of beads—the beads are all money, like wampum. Every time you want something, like a drink, or room service, or extra towels, or...sex—you just exchange one of your brightly colored beads for it.

NANO: (*Sitting on the edge of her bed, horrified*) Oh god, what are we coming to?

NICKI: Each of the Club Meds have their specialties— like some of them cater to three ways—

NANO: What?

NICKI: Three people at a time in bed.

(NANO *covers her mouth with her hand.*)

NICKI: Some are for homosexuals, some are for people who just like to watch—guess that's a sort of sister camp to one of the other ones—course not all of them are that—blatant—some are just all nudist, or vegetarian. And I read somewhere that they're thinking of starting one where none of the male guests can be *circumcised.*

(NICKI *watches* NANO *carefully for her reaction.*)

NANO: Oooouuh. It's disgusting. Why the thought of it—

NICKI: If I ever had a boy I sure wouldn't do it to him.

NANO: Ooooouuh. Don't even joke about it.

NICKI: I'm not.

NANO: But that's insane—

NICKI: Insane? You know what's insane? That for close to five thousand years an educated people could believe that if they took a knife to little baby boys they were fulfilling a covenant.

NANO: That's the way it's always been—

NICKI: It was not. Circumcision was forced on the Jews by the Egyptians—it was just their way of marking their slaves.

NANO: *(Shaking her head)* I don't know who you've been talking to, but—

NICKI: Everybody knows that, Nano. Some Harvard professor spent years in the fertile crescent researching the origin of the pre-sliced jelly roll and it is now undisputed *fact*.

NANO: *(Not so much shocked now as amused)* Nicki, I never heard such talk—

NICKI: Well, it's true.

NANO: Maybe so, but it's just good hygiene.

NICKI: That's just an old wives tale, Nano. If you can keep your hands and feet clean, and god knows where they end up going, you can keep that clean as well. *(She pauses, for effect.)* And anyway, it's a lot prettier if you don't do it.

NANO: And how would you know?

NICKI: *(Pause. Deliberately)* Pictures.

NANO: Pictures?

NICKI: Pictures.

NANO: Ooooouh, what are we coming to, animals? Do we have nothing better to do than run around sniffing each other like dogs? Everybody's obsessed with sex—sex sex sex. Well let me tell you there are more important things in a marriage than sex.

Companionship. That's what marriage is all about. A good marriage. There's nothing like that in the world.

NICKI: Suppose I'll have to worry about that first, circumcision later.

NANO: That would be the sensible thing to do.

Mamma lost a baby that way you know—he was the most perfect baby you ever saw. Just beautiful. And happy—you never saw such a happy little thing. Happy from the instant he was born. Joplin was a small town back then, and they had to bring a moile down from Kansas City for the ceremony—Mamma and Papa had a fight about it, she wanted it done by a doctor, but Papa's family had all come down, and they were more orthodox. And anyway Mamma was still in the hospital—in those days you stayed for almost two weeks, you didn't climb down off the delivery table and go back to work the way the women nowadays do. I remember going with Papa to meet the train— the moile was a short little ugly man, and Papa was so polite to him—a man who didn't speak a *word* of English. Well, the baby died the next day.
He was the most perfect baby I ever saw.

NICKI: What did your parents do?

NANO: Do? What could they do? They buried him.

NICKI: Couldn't they sue or—

NANO: You didn't *sue* in those days. (*Pause*) You just went on. (*Pause*) You'll feel differently about it when you get married, Nicki.

NICKI: Nope. I won't. I'll have it written into the prenuptial agreement.

(*There is a slight banging noise coming from the room on the other side of the wall behind the beds. The noise will grow, and will unmistakably be the sound of a couple making love.*)

NANO: Certain things are done—you can't up and say you won't do them—what kind of a world would we have it people did that!

NICKI: A world where babies don't have to be mutilated at birth—

NANO: What is wrong with you—

NICKI: Nothing is wrong with me. You just can't accept that there's a whole world going on out there that's not going to go away, no matter how hard you want it to.

NANO: There is nothing wrong with the way I've lead my life—nothing—

NICKI: I'm not saying there is, Nano, I'm saying that there isn't anything wrong with the way other people do. Premarital sex doesn't exist to upset you. Inflation wasn't invented to persecute you. People don't take their clothes off in the movies on the off chance that you might be in the audience and be outraged. They don't care what you think. So why should you care what they do? You just— (*Responding to the noise next door*) Oh great. Just great. You hear what they're doing in there?

NANO: I don't know and I don't care. It's none of my business.

NICKI: They might be married, Nano. Shouldn't upset you to hear it if they're married.

NANO: I have no apologies to make about my life— certainly not to you—

NICKI: All I'm saying is that everything that happens is not a personal attack on you—everyone who doesn't agree with you is not trying to take something from you—

NANO: I haven't lived my life just so you can tell me it's all wrong—

NICKI: I just want it to be easier for you—Nano—

(NANO *pulls away from* NICKI.)

NICKI: Nano listen to me—it would be easier for you,
you wouldn't be so upset all the time, if you'd just see
things the way they are—I know it's different from
the way it was when you grew up, I know that certain
things that maybe weren't right when you were my
age are hard for you, I know it's hard, but—

NANO: *(Screaming)* You want me to say it's all right
for you to sleep with whoever you want, this one this
week, another the next, like some tramp? You want me
to say that it's all right for people to have children right
and left, breeding like rabbits, never bothering to get
married? Well who do you think suffers—I'll tell you—
the little children do.
I can't say that everything I lived my life for means
nothing—that's what you want me to say—you want
me to say that all my values and morals are useless—
meaningless—you want me to say that it didn't matter
how I've lived BUT I CAN' T SAY IT!! I WON' T SAY
IT—leave me alone please, dear God, just leave me
alone.

NICKI: *(Crying)* Nano—please—I'm sorry—I didn't
mean it—Nano—

(NICKI *tries to hold* NANO, NANO *pushes her away.*)

NANO: Listen here young lady—you listen—we
will live our separate lives. You will always be my
granddaughter but this is finished—through—I can't
help loving you but I'll be damned if I will let you pick
and pick at me, telling me I don't know how to live
my life WELL I KNOW. It's my life, a good life, and
I'm not sorry about any of the things I did and why
I did them—I was a good daughter and a good wife
and a good mother and a damn good grandmother to
you three children and no one, *no one* is going to tell

me I wasn't. *(Exhausted, she falls on the bed weeping.)* Oh why did I come here—why did I come—I should never of left my house—I should have never come, I told myself, don't go, don't go, it will just be the same, you'll fight and fight, and I don't want to fight, I love you too much, and I let you talk me into it, and I do, I do want to come, I love you so, and then this, oh Nicki please, let this be the end of it, let's not to this to each other again, please. Let's just try to live out the rest of this trip as best we can, we'll be very careful, we'll be so careful of each other, and we won't ever attempt this again.

(NICKI lies on her bed, sobbing. NANO pulls the bed spread around her, and lies curled up on her bed.)

(The sounds from the next room crescendo, and then stop.)

(Time passes.)

(Light through the sliding glass doors gradually builds, as the sun rises.)

NANO: Nicki?

NICKI: Yes, Nano?

NANO: Are you awake? I didn't want to disturb you.

NICKI: Yes, I'm awake.

NANO: I thought it might be time to get up.

NICKI: We don't have to—we don't have far to go today.

NANO: Let's get as much driving done today as we can—get it over with. *(She goes into the bathroom.)*

NICKI: Okay.

NANO: *(O S)* If that's all right with you.

NICKI: Yes. It's fine. *(She gets off the bed, runs her fingers through her hair, and stands at the door.)* Ready?

NANO: *(Comes from the bathroom, ready to go)* Yes.

(NICKI holds the door for NANO, they leave.)

(The MAID enters, still humming Marching Through Georgia.*)*

(She makes the beds, reversing the bedspreads again.)

(She places a WELCOME TO MACON *sign on the T V and leaves.)*

(It is several moments before the door opens and NANO and NICKI enter.)

(NANO goes into the bathroom, to change.)

(NICKI gets some things from her overnight bag, and sits on the edge of her bed, waiting for NANO to come out of the bathroom.)

(NANO enters from the bathroom, adjusting her helmet. NICKI goes into the bathroom to change.)

(NANO carefully turns down her bed, then looks at NICKI's bed, turns hers down neatly too. She sighs, gets into bed.)

(By the time NICKI enters from the bathroom, dressed for bed, NANO is already—or pretending to be—asleep.)

(NICKI sees that NANO has turned down the bed, looks at NANO, smiles sadly, gets into bed and turns off the light.)

(The light grows, through the sliding glass doors.)

(NANO and NICKI get up, and go to the bathroom.)

(The MAID enters, humming the Mickey Mouse Theme *song, somewhat mournfully.)*

(She places Mickey Mouse ears on the desk, the phone, and puts a Mickey Mouse WELCOME TO ORLANDO *sign on the T V.)*

(The MAID then remakes the beds, turning them down, placing a small candy on the pillows. She leaves.)

(NANO emerges from the bathroom, adjusting her helmet. She sits down on her bed, eats her candy, and gets into bed.)

(NICKI *comes over to her bed. She eats her candy, then gets into bed. She turns off the light, goes to sleep.*)

(*After some moments,* NANO *begins to cry in her sleep. She sounds as though she might be in pain—and she calls out a name, just barely intelligibly.*)

NANO: Richard...Richard...oh God, oh God, Richard—

(NICKI *wakes, listening. She gets out of bed and leans over* NANO's *bed.*)

NICKI: *(Whispering)* Nano—Nano you all right—

NANO: Richard—oh God, oh, oh—

NICKI: Nano—please—are you all—

(NICKI *touches her softly,* NANO *wakes.*)

NANO: What's wrong?

NICKI: Nothing, I'm sorry—I just—

NANO: I wasn't snoring, was I? Nicki, you must tell me if I'm snoring—I'll be very upset with you if you don't—

NICKI: No, Nano, you weren't.

NANO: I must have been dreaming—I never dream anymore, only when I'm with you. And then they're so crazy— they don't make any sense.

NICKI: You were—calling his name.

NANO: Oh. Haven't done that in years.

NICKI: When I was little you used to do it all the time.

NANO: Yes, I always felt so terrible, keeping you up at night. But I couldn't help myself—I had to have you children with me after he died, I had to.
The house was so terribly lonely then.

NICKI: I was only what—eleven? —twelve? —and I was terrified. I don't know of what, but I knew there was something that waited just outside your bedroom

door, that waited for me to fall asleep. There were
nights I could hear it breathing. I don't know what I
thought would happen, if I fell asleep and it came in—
but I knew that something horrible had happened once
and I couldn't let it happen again. It had happened to
him, in the twin bed next to you and it was my job to
guard you, to make sure it didn't happen again.

NANO: The hardest part was watching all the men
come home from work and go out to pick up their
papers, all the way up and down the block. I couldn't
make myself go out then—I couldn't—walk down that
long driveway of mine, walk up all alone again with
that paper. So I just sat and waited till I could. There's
not so much to miss in a newspaper now-a-days
anyway, lot of nonsense.
They've got a new paper boy on the route now—I'll
call and cancel my subscription he doesn't stop
throwing it on the roof. And when it's not on the roof
it's in the rose bushes.

NICKI: I tried so hard to keep you safe.

NANO: Now I go out and hunt for my paper—I don't
even notice what the weather is. And it used to be
my favorite time of day—I used to love to sit by the
window, the way Mamma and I had done when I was
a little girl, listening to the birds sing, waiting for him
to come home.

NICKI: I wish I remembered him better.

NANO: He adored you children.

NICKI: You know the only thing I remember—I
remember how he would come in and bless us when
we spent the night at your house, before we went to
sleep. (She struggles to remember the blessing.) May the
Lord bless you...may the Lord be gracious unto you...
may the Lord— (She raises her hands in the position of the
priestly blessing—fore and index fingers together, third and

little finger together, making a "V" in the center.) —lift up
His countenance upon you, and give you peace. *(She
looks at her hands, lowers them slightly, and says, in a deep
voice:)* Live long and prosper.

NANO: It's a lovely prayer, isn't it.

NICKI: That last part's from *Star Trek*, Nano.

NANO: What—oh, one of those T V shows you
children used to watch. *(Laughing softly)* He always
called you his little ray of sunshine, you know, and he
always used to look at you and say "Nicki may be the
youngest, but she'll be the one to marry first. She'll be
the first of our girls to walk down the aisle."

NICKI: He did?

NANO: Yes, but he was right about a lot of other things.

NICKI: Do you still miss him?

NANO: Terribly. He died too young.

NICKI: It's almost twenty years now.

NANO: Doesn't seem possible, does it.

NICKI: You know, Nano, I've been thinking about
it, and I've decided. I'm going to marry someone
younger.

NANO: Well, at the rate you're going, you won't have
much choice. All your contemporaries will have died
of old age.

NICKI: I could go as low as twenty-five—that would
be all right— 'course, he'd still be five years past his
sexual peak, but sex isn't everything, right?

NANO: Oh, Nicki, when you have a good marriage,
there's nothing like it in the world. That's why I'm so
hipped on your getting married. It's just you and him
and nobody can take that away from you. *(She holds out*

her arms and holds NICKI.*)* Oh, Nicki, I want so much for
you—

NICKI: I know, Nano, I know—

NANO: If you knew how I looked forward to our trips
together—

NICKI: Next year it will be better, Nano, we won't fight,
I promise—

NANO: No, Nicki, it just won't do.

NICKI: But I promise—

NANO: Then what would we find to do? I like fighting,
occasionally. You're too much like me not to like it too.
No, that's not why I don't think we should ever
attempt this again.

NICKI: Nano, please don't—

NANO: If you knew how I lie in bed at night, trying to
think what to do with you.

NICKI: No wonder you're so tired—no wonder you
can't make it through the day—

NANO: That has nothing to do with it and you know it.

NICKI: You'd be just fine if you didn't keep yourself up
worrying all the time.

NANO: WELL SOMEONE HAS TO.

NICKI: *(Pause)* Why?

NANO: Because.

NICKI: It doesn't do anybody any good.

NANO: All the same, I do it, Nicki. I lie in my bed at
night and I cross my fingers, and I say a prayer for you.

NICKI: I know you do.

NANO: I just wish I was doing a better job of it, that's
all.

NICKI: So do I. But until then—

NANO: I'd do anything in the world for you, Nicki. You know that, don't you?
Anything in the world. *(She kisses* NICKI.*)* Now let's get some sleep. We'll be in Boca tomorrow morning.

NICKI: Nano?

NANO: Yes, dear?

*(*NICKI *holds her.)*

(It grows gradually lighter—morning.)

(The MAID *enters as* NANO *and* NICKI *go into the bathroom to change.)*

(She is humming Meet Me In Saint Louis, Louis.*)*

(The MAID *takes away the Mickey Mouse ears, flips the pictures back to Monets, replaces the lampshades, puts a* WELCOME TO SAINT LOUIS *sign on the T V, and leaves.)*

*(*NICKI *emerges from the bathroom and begins putting her nightgown, etc, away in her overnight bag.)*

NICKI: I'm ready anytime you are.

NANO: *(O S)* Just think—I'll be back in my own bed tonight— *(Sticks her head out the bathroom door)* What bliss! *(Claps her hands, goes back into the bathroom.)* Well, I'm not saying it was a bad trip but it wasn't exactly a great one. Too bad it's our last one.

NICKI: Nano—

NANO: All right, I'm not saying it was torture, it wasn't, exactly, but—

NICKI: You don't mean it, Nano.

NANO: I most certainly do.
You are the thing I love most in my life, Nicki, but there's no point in us going on with these trips.

NICKI: I'M SORRY WE FIGHT. I SAID I WAS SORRY.

NANO: Oh, good Lord, Nicki, it's not the fighting—

NICKI: I don't mean to fight, I try so hard—

NANO: Well, you're certainly putting on a good imitation.
People don't bother fighting about things that don't matter to them, with people they don't think are important.

NICKI: Okay, I do want to fight with you. But just because it's important for you to see things the way the way they are.

NANO: In your opinion.

NICKI: Well, sure, in my opinion, but—

NANO: You'd be a mealy mouthed thing if you didn't think your opinion was the gospel truth. So would I. Which is why *I* have no intention of seeing things any different from the way they really are, too.

NICKI: But I just want to protect you—to help you to—

NANO: I'm not the person you should be fighting with, Nicki.

NICKI: Maybe, but since you *are* the person I'm fighting with—

NANO: There is someone out there, some nice man whose life you should be making a living hell instead.

NICKI: No. I don't think there is.

NANO: Don't be ridiculous—

NICKI: I think some people only get one perfect relationship, Nano. They only get one. I got you.

NANO: *(Pause)* Don't talk like that.

NICKI: And anyway, who says these fights would be good if they were with my husband, but they—what—

have no value because they're with you? Who says that?

NANO: Everybody says that.

NICKI: I don't.

NANO: I do. And I have company. The whole rest of the world.

NICKI: So what? Can't I be right? Can't the whole rest of the world be wrong?

NANO: You know you're wrong, if you'd just stop pretending—

NICKI: I'm not pretending—

NANO: It's not an ideal world. You can't have things the way you want them just because you've decided that's the way they should be.

NICKI: That— *(Pause)* That's my line. That's what I say to you. *(Pause)* What if you find something perfect, Nano. What if you find something perfect, and it isn't perfect, the way somebody else would find it, but it is to you? Then you have every right to hang on to it. To fight for it.

NANO: There's nothing sadder than an old maid, Nicki—

NICKI: That is *just* the kind of thinking that has to change.

NANO: Why should it change, Nicki, it's the truth. You feminists can pretend all you want that it's otherwise, but everybody knows it's all a sham.

NICKI: I *hate* it when you talk like this—

NANO: Because you know it's true—

NICKI: *(Starts to yell)* Nano. *(Then stops herself)*

NANO: Nicki.

NICKI: I'm not going to settle, Nano. Oceans and oceans and not one drop less.

NANO: Then you'll be alone all your life, Nicki.

NICKI: No I won't. I have you.

NANO: Nicki, I am—

NANO/NICKI: —a decrepit old woman.

NICKI: So what? I am going to make sure you live forever.

NANO: Nicki, don't joke about it.

NICKI: All right. Even if you don't—
I'll always have you.

NANO: *(Softly)* It won't be enough.

NICKI: Millions of people do with less.

NANO: But you don't have to, Nicki, you have—

NANO/NICKI: —so much to give.

NANO: Which is why you've got to find yourself a husband to fight with. How hard can it be? Someone who's not perfect, maybe, but has a few redeeming qualities, maybe a nice doctor, they make a good income and they're never underfoot at home, they're so busy you're lucky if you can remember what they look like. *(Pause)* Now listen to me. I've had a lot of time to think this trip, and I've realized something. I've made up my mind. And you know what it means when I make up my mind.
As long as I keep holding on to you, you're not going to notice you need someone else to hold. I know. I've seen this happen before, with your Aunt Sadie and your Uncle Irving—they were needed at home, and it was so safe and comfortable there, and Mamma and Papa needed them, and it's good to feel needed, it's good to be there, to give, and take care, but one day

they both woke up old and alone. It would kill me if it happened to you.

NICKI: I *hate* it when you compare me to Aunt Sadie. She was afraid of life, and she made being picky into an art form, and—

NANO: I have made up my mind, Nicki. My mind's made up. I know we both pretend I'm not just a decrepit old woman who needs someone to take her south out of the cold every year, but there's got to be an end to it.

What a selfish old woman I must look like. Well, I'm not going to selfish any longer. We've had one last good trip. We'll be able to remember it for along time. I want you to have someone to take you south some day, Nicki—when you can't take yourself, when all the people you've known are gone, and there is nothing left of all the world you knew—I want you to have a granddaughter to carry you south someday too.

(NANO *and* NICKI *hold each other for a moment.*)

NANO: Well. Never thought I'd live to see the day I'd miss a Howard Johnson's motel room. All this hideous orange and turquoise blue. Ooooooooooh.

NICKI: That's okay—I'm taking along a little souvenir— (*She pulls the corner of an orange and blue bordered bath mat out of her overnight bag.*)

NANO: (*Horrified*) NICKI! You put that back!

NICKI: Why, Nano—they expect you to take a towel or two—

NANO: That's stealing—

NICKI: (*Hurries out the door*) That's why they have their name on it—advertising—

NANO: What are we coming to— (*Following* NICKI *out the door*) What is the matter with you people—NICKI—

NICKI: *(As the door swings shut)* There is nothing the matter with *me*, Nano—

NANO: *(O S)* I never heard of such a thing—come back here young lady—Nicki—NICKI!!!

(A beat)

(NANO storms back in with the bathmat, puts it in the bathroom.)

(As she passes by the ice bucket, she hesitates. She picks it up. Puts it back down. Then picks it up and puts it in her pocketbook. It fits.)

(She gives a little shrug and a smile, and leaves.)

(Blackout)

END OF PLAY

www.ingramcontent.com/pod-product-compliance
Lightning Source LLC
Chambersburg PA
CBHW052219090426

42741CB00010B/2602